The Dust is Golden

— Haiku —

Jackie Hardy

First published in 1999 by IRON Press
5 Marden Terrace
Cullercoats
North Shields
Northumberland
NE30 4PD, UK
Tel/Fax: (0191) 253 1901

Typeset in Elan 12pt by Jack Lithgow

Printed by Peterson Printers, South Shields

© Copyright Jackie Hardy 1999

Front cover paintings by Nicola Balfour

Cover and Book design by Peter Mortimer

ISBN 0 906228 72 7

IRON Press books are represented by
Signature Book Representation
Sun House, 2 Little Peter Street
Manchester M15 4PS
Tel: (0161) 834 8767
Fax: (0161) 834 8656
e-mail: admin@signature-books.co.uk

Contents

9
Making Sense

11
Days

18
The wood from the trees

20
Months

29
Chance

31
Here

33
There

35
Anywhere

37
7.50 from Hexham

Acknowledgements

Acknowledgements are due to the editors of the following publications in which some of these poems first appeared:
Bare Bones, Blithe Spirit, Haiku Spirit (Eire), Haiku World: An International Poetry Almanac (USA), Ko (Japan), New Welsh Review, Presence, the old moon and so on (New Zealand Poetry Society Anthology), The Haiku Seasons: Poetry of the Natural World (USA), Vuursteen (Netherlands), Yellow Moon (Australia).

THE DUST IS GOLDEN

JACKIE HARDY

Lives in Northumberland, a county which has inspired many of her haiku. Between 1993 and 1997 she was the editor of the British Haiku Society's journal, *Blithe Spirit*. Her haiku has been published in seven countries and translated into several languages. She writes in various poetic forms and her first collection, *Counting the Waves* was published by Bloodaxe in 1998.

For Polly & Daniel

"The days and months are travellers of eternity."
Matsuo Basho

(The Narrow Road to the Deep North,
translated by Nobuyuki Yuasa)

Making Sense

across the meadow
   wind ripples the grasses
     warm breath on her neck

   summer's first rose
     inhaling the bouquet
       of his sweat

    sea spray
      veiling the cliff
         salt's tang on her lips

*

from a glass vase
   a fall of wisteria
      low sound in her throat

spring dawn -
   his withdrawing member
      still glistening

Days

summer dawn -
a blackbird gads in
and out of the haar

smoothing paper
on my fingertips
the roughness of words

clearing cloud
through cedar branches
the slope of the fell

dusk -
the lake water so still
will o' the wisp

*

dawn chorus
above the small birds' treble
soprano peacock

map reading -
turns out to be just a hill
Roseberry Topping

winter afternoon:
between the swish of wet tyres
pop music, needling

full moon
from deep in the sycamore
the hoots of an owl

*

good news in the post:
my breakfast porridge
grows a skin

cremation day:
alone for the first time
the neighour's dog howls

a soft light
falling on surfinias
summer rain

a sudden wakening
in such blackness -
the night of no moon

*

thunderstorm at dawn
between lightning flashes
counting car alarms

out walking alone
just as I think of her
a friend turns the bend

evening -
the herd heads gatewards
the traffic thins

behind thin clouds
the full moon's brilliance
a child sleeping

*

sleepless again
Odysseus nears Ithaca
the darkness fades

low tide -
to and fro in the rock pool
frisbee reflections

afternoon downpour -
traffic
rattles the windows

after long hot days
reluctantly
the night

*

morning -
the bedside light, my specs
still on

ebb tide;
sea belt clinches
the rocks

off shore breeze -
dry sand sidewinding
the deserted beach

low sun -
moving in the next field
my shadow

*

Sunday morning
fingers read teethmarks
in the headlines

discovered
watching adult videos
the heat of her lips

in the Plough's taproom
furrows on his face fade
as the bitter clears

after the party ...
a large deposit
at the bottle bank

The Wood from the Trees

*October sun -
through the shadows' chill
this year's last outing*

>   *such a still day -
>   from the ridge top
>   the creak of a pine*

>   *sculpture trail -
>   not making head or tail
>   of this hand-smoothed wood*

*

stone fox -
how warm one red flank
how cold the other

on a pine trunk
the tall black shadow
of another pine

Months

> *cold wind from the east*
> *in a damaged spider's web*
> *a red leaf shivers*

listening
to the forest's silence
the drip, drip
of melting snow

> *through falling snow*
> *the oak tree's outline*
> *barely moving*

*

day-long rain -
on the telegraph wire
one drop forms, one drips

frosty fields -
on the fingerpost
a lone crow

days into the thaw
still lodged on top of the pond
stones

*

catkins -
around the vase
the dust is golden

above stick nests
weaving a spiral flight
the caw of rooks

walking through the flock
between the lambs' bleats
no sound

*

blackthorn -
in the first burst of blossom
a shrivelled sloe

spring snow -
on scumbled slopes
a scattering of lambs

heavy rain -
on a pock-marked cowpat
a drowned fly

*

fresh May wind
   cherry blossom
      darkens in drifts

      in a sunbeam
   a bluebottle speeds up
     floating motes

a dock leaf
missed by the mower
spins in the wind

*

summer's first heat
in the lid of your sunscreen
scrunch of last year's beach

dog roses over
on the verge
rose bay willow herb

summer evening -
round the bay empty deckchairs
looking out to sea

*

in a passing car
just time to see
the batsman, out

        railway cutting -
        rose bay willow herb
        pinking the banks

school holidays -
cloud shadows and children
race along the sands

*

in the lay-by
tethered in gypsy lace
the travellers' horse

eve of the twelfth:
I'm up on the moors
advising the grouse

hot summer night
music from an open window
a clap of thunder

*

in still air
rising smoke from the bonfire
bisects the sky

horizontal sun -
dark against the dazzle
the fleeing deer

frost warning -
those delicate plants
humming with bees

*

patches of mist
lingering along the road
a child late for school

      in the wooded dene
        a leaf plunges
        into the sound
        of water

north wind
    a sudden gust
        kaleidoscopes
            the fallen leaves

*

rain from the north
face down
the fallen scarecrow

Remembrance Day
silently the moving flags
cherry tree's last leaf

winter dusk -
a distant train whistle
wind from the north

*

*cold hands
deep in my coat pocket
a forgotten coin*

*a winter oak:
unshed leaves
rustle*

*Boxing Day meet -
hounds mooch around
protestors' legs*

Chance

you stand
framed in my window
moonlight through the trees

stars;
the wind swings the shutters,
again those stars

midnight
your thumb strums my nipple
a creak on the stair

*

waking alone,
beside the bed
forgotten shoes

      across the valley
      the last roll of thunder
      cloud wisps from the trees

Here

>   *through stained glass*
>   *sunlight rainbows*
>   *the mongrel's coat*

walkers on the ridge -
in the valley their shadows
keeping step

>   *Stanhope Moor:*
>   *miles and miles of fence*
>   *divides the heather*

on the carcass
cutting it fine
crow in the road

>*valley walk*
>*between the train's whistle*
>*and its echo*

country road
the shooting syndicate's car
gunning it

There

> *in Belfast Lough*
> *the wavering reflections*
> *red winter sun*

cold on Cave Hill
envying seagulls
riding the thermals

> *a stiff breeze*
> *on Killington Lake*
> *one red sail*

High Force -
over the thunder of water
a cuckoo calls

    duty free
    on the Paris flight
    below glass winks

        Bass Rock
        at the end of the rainbow
        buttoning my mac

Anywhere

*driving rain -
behind the huddle of sheep
a dry stone wall*

*spooked by laughter
a flock of gulls
ghosts the mist*

*caught short:
above the sound of my stream
a curlew calls*

on a unseen thread
a leaf spins
in a sudden draught

new building site
stripped to the bare essentials
brown backs, tattoos

photocall -
grandchildren at his knee
he cradles his son

7.50 from Hexham

Early morning. Early autumn. The train was late. But only a few minutes and I didn't mind today. Today, there was no hurry. I'd made this journey from Hexham to Carlisle many times, but this was my first time by rail. When the train pulled in, I was the only passenger to board. I selected a seat facing forward, relaxed into it and waited to experience a different perspective.

from the train window
the villages I know
only by road

The first part of the journey tracks the upper reaches of the River Tyne, before it splits into the North and South Tynes. This morning, in the sunshine, the valley was at its best: the river swift, woods tinged with yellows, the distant hills. I congratulated myself on the decision to live alongside it, enjoying the twists and turns of the Tyne which remain invisible from the road.

sunlight
on that stretch of the river
seen for the first time

I pondered on the choices we make. Why had I chosen to travel by rail today?

> *reflecting -*
> *seeing myself*
> *in the darkened glass*

How one route we take in life excludes another; one route may be narrow and confined,

> *in the cutting*
> *fireweed seeds*
> *gust in the wind*

another opens up new vistas, ideas.

*identifying
hawthorns high on the fell,
their red berries*

Thinking about some of the choices I have made in the past, I took a pilgrimage along the what-might-have-been way. What if had taken that road to employment, that quiet lane to a relationship, that motorway to freedom? This train of thought made me aware how abundant this valley is in history. The Romans lived and built here; notorious reivers fought over sheep, cattle, women; the fortunes and houses of prominent families rose and fell.

on Hadrian's Wall
fenced off now,
a crow perches

castle ruins
in and out of arrow slits
jackdaws

The train crossed the border from grey-stoned Northumberland to Cumbria where the houses are built of a more cheerful red sandstone. Are the Cumbrians more ebullient people than the dour Northumbrians, I wondered, because of geology? How much does where we live influence what happens in our lives? Perhaps very little. Perhaps it's more important to be ready to take advantage of what comes along; be able to recognise life chances when they happen. Be prepared.

Suddenly, the track passes over a steep ravine, the River Eden in the bottom, a hundred feet below. The train clattered into the overgrown station at Wetherall where children gathered blackberries on the platform.

no longer used
the station master's house
climbed by sweet peas

Obeying a red signal, the train halted outside the station at Carlisle. As I looked out at the city suburbs and the shunting yards, I noticed that here the people were looking ahead, at least to winter. Getting prepared.

> *waiting -*
> *　　in the siding*
> *a snow plough*

> *　　　storage depot -*
> *　　　a digger moves coal*
> *　　　one pile to the next*

*　　　* * * * **